STUDYING WEATHER

WEATHER REPORT

Ann and Jim Merk

The Rourke Corporation, Inc.
Vero Beach, Florida 32964

PHOTO CREDITS
© Lynn M. Stone: title page, pages 4, 7, 8, 10, 13, 17, 21; courtesy
National Oceanic and Atmospheric Administration: cover; courtesy
NASA: page 15; courtesy South Dakota Tourism: page 12; courtesy
University of Wisconsin, Department of Meteorology: page 18

Library of Congress Cataloging-in-Publication Data

Merk, Ann, 1952–
    Studying weather / by Ann and Jim Merk.
      p. cm. — (Weather report)
    Includes index
    ISBN 0-86593-385-5
    1. Weather—Juvenile literature. 2. Meteorology—Juvenile
literature.   [1. Weather 2. Meteorology.]
I. Merk, Jim, 1952- . II. Title   III. Series: Merk, Ann, 1952- Weather
report.
QC981.3.M53 1994
551.5—dc20   94-13320
                                    CIP
Printed in the USA   AC

TABLE OF CONTENTS

STUDYING WEATHER

The "way it is outside" is important to everyone. **Weather** is the way it is outside on any day at any time. It could be hot, cold, wet, dry, windy or calm.

Weather helps people make choices—what to do, where to go, what to wear and even what to grow.

People who study weather are **meteorologists**. Part of their job is to learn more about how weather works. Another part of their job is to predict the weather.

Weather conditions help people decide what to do, what to wear

STUDYING CLIMATE

Climate is the weather of any place over a long period of time. An area's climate depends largely upon its rainfall and temperatures.

Scientists keep records on the climate and study them. By studying climate, scientists can predict whether an area will be good for growing certain crops.

Scientists also study climate to look for changes. But because real changes in climate occur only over many years, scientists often disagree about whether an area's climate has changed.

A dry climate shapes the way that plants and animals live in the desert

METEOROLOGISTS

Benjamin Franklin was one of the founders of the United States in the 1770's. He was also one of the first people to study weather in North America.

Today's meteorologists have far more special education and special equipment than Mr. Franklin had. These weather scientists predict tomorrow's weather and also weather in the more distant future.

A meteorologist at the University of Wisconsin (Madison) gathers weather information from a computer system

MEASURING WEATHER

To make their predictions, weather scientists study and measure weather conditions. A scientist must measure the weight of the air. The scientist must measure the temperature of the air, ground and water. In addition, weather scientists measure **humidity**, or moisture, in the air.

They also measure wind speed and direction, and they measure **precipitation**—rainfall and snowfall.

A thermometer measures air temperature, and this thermometer shows that it is still winter in the Rockies

Weather forecasts and severe storm warnings help people avoid dangerous weather

The signals of weather satellites are picked up by "dishes"—receivers—at weather stations

WEATHER INSTRUMENTS

Weather scientists gather information from many sources—satellites, computers, weather stations and people who observe weather.

Some of the instruments that measure weather conditions are commonly used by people other than scientists.

A **barometer**, for instance, measures the weight, or pressure, of air masses. Changes in the barometer mean a change in the weather.

A thermometer measures air temperature. A rain gauge measures the amount of rain. **Anemometers** measure the speed of wind.

Scientists inspect a weather satellite before launch at the Kennedy Space Center, Florida

WEATHER STATIONS

Weather stations are places where instruments gather information about weather. Weather stations are set up throughout the world.

Weather stations may have people working in them, or they may be "packages" of instruments that operate themselves.

Some weather stations float on oceans. Others are buildings or satellites. Weather satellites send photos and information to weather stations on the ground.

Chains anchor a weather station on Mount Washington, New Hampshire, where hurricane force winds are common

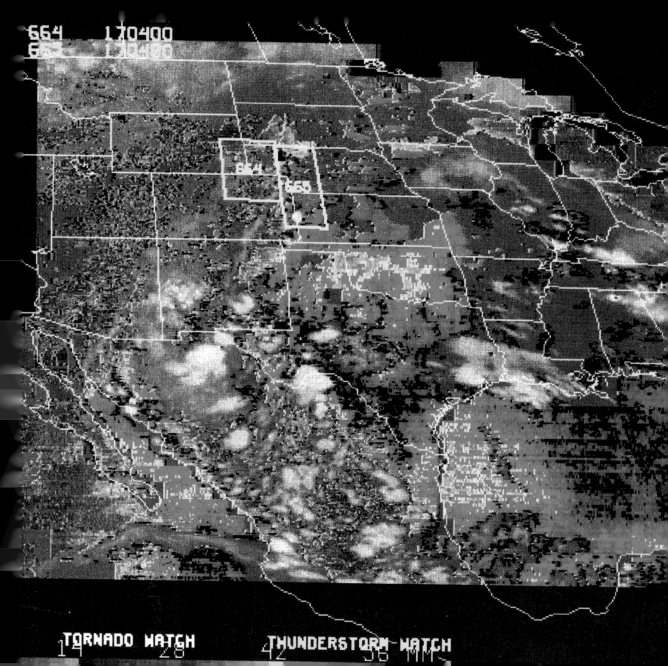

WEATHER MAPS

Weather maps help people see weather conditions over a broad area. They show storms, temperatures, and the location of large systems of weather called **fronts**.

A front is a boundary between a mass of cold air and a mass of warmer air. As fronts move into an area, the weather changes.

Weather maps help **forecasters**, the people who predict how the weather will change.

Computers print detailed weather maps from satellite signals

MAKING WEATHER FORECASTS

Weather forecasters try to determine what future weather will be. Forecasters feed information about weather conditions into computers. A computer can tell a forecaster what happened in the past with similar weather conditions. Once a forecaster knows what happened in the past and is happening in the present, then the big test comes: What will happen next?

Computer operators in the Department of Meteorology at the University of Wisconsin gather weather information from around the world

WHY STUDY THE WEATHER?

We study weather for many reasons. One is that we are curious. By studying weather conditions today, we often know what kind of weather to expect tomorrow.

We also study weather to find out if the Earth's climate—its weather over a long period of time—is changing. If it is, we need to know why. Changing weather could have an impact—for better or worse—on everyone.

Glossary

anemometer (an uh MOM eh ter) — an instrument for measuring wind speed

barometer (bar OHM uh ter) — an instrument that measures the pressure, or weight, of air

climate (KLI mit) — the type of weather conditions that any place has over a long period of time

forecaster (FOR kas ter) — one who predicts, especially the weather

front (FRONT) — the boundary between two different air masses

humidity (hu MID ih tee) — wetness or moisture in the air

meteorologist (meet e uh RAHL uh gist) — a scientist who studies the Earth's atmosphere and its weather

precipitation (pre sip uh TAY shun) — rain, snow and sleet

weather (WEH ther) — what it is like outside on any day at any time

INDEX

551.5
Mer

Merk, Ann, 1952-
Studying weather

DATE DUE	BORROWER	

551.5
Mer

Merk, Ann, 1952-
Studying weather

Anderson Elementary

 GUMDROP BOOKS - Bethany, Missouri